Trudi Parkes

A Family Guide to
Pray for the World

40 Days more
40 Bites

40 Days more 40 Bites

more

A Family Guide to Pray for the World

Trudi Parkes

10 9 8 7 6 5 4 3 2 1

© Copyright 2017 Trudi Parkes

ISBN: 978-1-5271-0039-8

Published in 2017 by Christian Focus Publications, Geanies House, Fearn, Tain, Ross-shire, IV20 1TW , U.K.

Cover design by Daniel van Straaten

Printed and bound in Malta

Scriptures quoted from the International Children's Bible, New Century Version [Anglicised Edition] Copyright © 1991 by Nelson Word Ltd, Milton Keynes, England. Used by permission.

Scripture quotations [marked NIV] taken from The Holy Bible, New International Version [Anglicised edition] Copyright © 1979, 1984, 2011 by Biblica. Used by permission of Hodder & Stoughton Publishers, an Hachette U.K. company. All rights reserved. 'NIV' is a registered trademark of Biblica. U.K. trademark number 1448790.

Population figures for countries are based on estimates from 'World Population Prospects: 2015 Revision' by the Population Division, Department of Economic and Social Affairs, United Nations. Figures over ten million have been rounded to the nearest million; countries under ten million have been rounded to the nearest hundred thousand; and countries under one million to the nearest thousand.

USE THIS GUIDE TO PRAY FOR THE WORLD
EVERY DAY FOR 40 DAYS
OR ONCE A WEEK ON A SPECIAL DAY!

THIS BOOK BELONGS TO

AND I AM GOING TO PRAY FOR THE WORLD!

CONTENTS

Day 1: Madagascar.............................8

Day 2: Toilets 10

Day 3: Greece 12

Day 4: Homeless People.....................14

Day 5: Greenland 16

Day 6: Persecution..........................18

Day 7: Egypt.................................20

Day 8: Floods................................22

Day 9: Maldives.............................24

Day 10: Aviation Ministry 26

Day 11: South Korea 28

Day 12: Child Trafficking..................30

Day 13: Saudi Arabia 32

Day 14: Creation Care.......................34

Day 15: Colombia 36

Day 16: Cities 38

Day 17: Brazil 40

Day 18: HIV/AIDS............................42

Day 19: France 44

Day 20: Hunger 46

Day 21: South Africa.........................50

Day 22: Orphans 52

Day 23: The Gambia...........................54

Day 24: Judaism 56

Day 25: Bhutan 58

Day 26: Addictions 60

Day 27: Afghanistan 62

Day 28: Hui in China 64

Day 29: New Zealand 66

Day 30: Hinduism...............................68

Day 31: Nepal.....................................70

Day 32: Europe 72

Day 33: Vietnam 74

Day 34: Roma People 76

Day 35: Somalia 78

Day 36: Unreached People Groups 80

Day 37: Sri Lanka 82

Day 38: Diaspora 84

Day 39: Indonesia 86

Day 40: Missionaries...........................88

DAY 1: MADAGASCAR

What do you think of when you hear the country Madagascar mentioned? Do you immediately think of Alex the lion, Marty the zebra or the cute penguins from the animated movies set in Madagascar? Some people may think of its famous vanilla which it grows and sells to other countries. Madagascar, however, is also known for being the fourth largest island in the world.

> "'You must worship the Lord your God. Serve only him!'"
> Matthew 4:10

It's about the size of France and is found about 250 miles off the coast of south-east Africa. Madagascar is a particularly interesting country because of its wildlife. Many of the plants and animals in Madagascar are not found anywhere else in the world. However, although it's rich in wildlife, it is one of the poorest countries in the world and so its people face many problems.

Over 200 years ago two men and their families went as missionaries to Madagascar. Sadly they all died within a few months except for one man called David Jones. Bravely, David did not give up but continued telling Madagascans about Jesus, many of whom became Christians. Later he also helped to translate the Bible into the Malagasy language.

Today many people in Madagascar still follow Jesus. However, some want to worship or pray to other gods and ancestral spirits as well as be a Christian. We know that this doesn't work and that God wants us to worship and serve only him.

PRAY

• Thank God for the first missionaries to Madagascar.

• For Madagascan Christians to only worship Jesus.

FACT FILE:

Population: 24 million

Main Religion: Christianity

Capital: Antananarivo

Official Languages: Malagasy and French

NEW WORD:

* Ancestral spirits: spirits of dead relatives.

DID YOU KNOW?

Madagascar is the only country where lemurs [like King Julien in the movie] can be found in the wild! There are around 100 different kinds of lemurs living there!

ON THE MAP

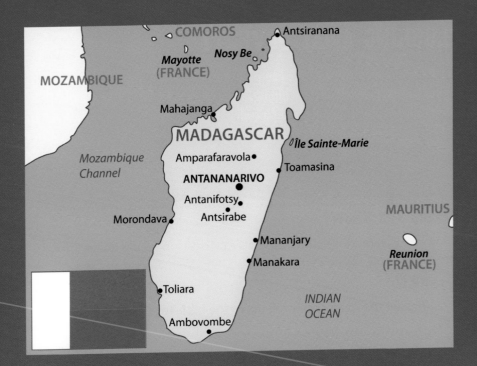

DAY 2: TOILETS

Imagine what life would be like if you didn't have a toilet at home. What would you do when you needed the loo? You might have to go in your garden. Or in a bucket in your bedroom. What do you think your house would smell like? Would your garden be a nice place to play?

IT'S OUT OF ORDER!

Do you know that about 2.4 billion people do not have a toilet? This means that about a third of the world's population have to use fields, rivers, roadsides, plastic bags or buckets. This can cause germs to spread and people to become sick or even die. Almost 900 children die every day from diseases caused by not having a proper toilet or clean water. That's one child every two minutes.

FLUSHING AWAY POVERTY

So what can we do to help? We can pray and we can give money to organisations such as Toilet Twinning. They work with local churches and communities to help people build a toilet and to teach them about hygiene such as washing their hands.

DID YOU KNOW?

Over a lifetime, it's estimated the average person spends about three years sitting on a toilet!

JOKE!

Why did the toilet paper roll down the hill? To get to the bottom!

MEET NIVA

Niva is fourteen and lives in India. She and her family now have a toilet, thanks to Toilet Twinning. She says, 'Before, we used to go to the toilet in the fields and we had lots of problems. All the ladies in the family used to go out together at about 5.30 a.m. But I worried about snake bites and I don't like the dark'.

PRAY

- For more poor people like Niva to be able to have a toilet to use.

- For those without a toilet to be protected from diseases.

GET INTO IT!

Get a collecting box from Toilet Twinning and fill it with money until you reach £60 ($77). Send the money to Toilet Twinning who will use it to help provide a toilet somewhere in the world. You will receive a certificate with a photo of the toilet you've twinned with, so you can then display it proudly.

DAY 3: GREECE

Greece is a mountainous country and has many islands, with Crete and Rhodes being the largest ones. Some people go to Greece on holiday because of its beautiful beaches, islands, ancient ruins and pretty villages on hills. Greece has influenced the world over thousands of years through its art, science and, especially, philosophy.

> 'He said, "Men of Athens, I can see that you are very religious in all things…You worship a god that you don't know."'
> Acts 17: 22-23

Greece is also famous for its Christian history. It was the first country in Europe to hear the gospel; the original New Testament was written in Greek and some of the New Testament letters were written to cities in Greece such as Philippi and Corinth. Today Greeks say they are religious and believe in God. Most belong to the Greek Orthodox Church and use pictures called icons, statues and candles to worship God. Sadly, however, many don't go to church often and few have a relationship with God or know Jesus as their friend and Saviour. Greece has many immigrants regularly arriving in its country, mainly because it's located between Europe, Asia, North Africa and the Middle East. The immigrants are looking for a better future and many have never heard about Jesus.

PRAY

• That Greeks in the Greek Orthodox Church would come into a living relationship with Jesus.

• That immigrants in Greece would find hope and a better future in God.

DID YOU KNOW?

The Olympics first started in the Greek town of Olympia in the eighth century B.C. It only had one event then – a 200 metre race!

NEW WORDS:

* Philosophy: a set of ideas, principles or beliefs. * Icon: a painting of Christ, his mother, or a saint. * Immigrant: someone who comes to live in a country from another country.

ON THE MAP

DAY 4: HOMELESS PEOPLE

> 'God will have a house for us to live in...It will be a home in heaven that will last forever.'
> 2 Corinthians 5:1

Homeless people don't have a home to live in and so sleep on pavements, in doorways, in parks and under bridges. Imagine having to sleep on the street feeling hungry and unsafe, with everything you own in one bag. How would you be able to wash, dress, and get work or study? What if you were ill?

There are about 100 million people throughout the world who are completely homeless. Some of them are children. This is on top of around 1.6 billion people who live in inadequate housing, for example, in slum areas.

There are many different reasons why people are homeless including poverty, unemployment, physical or mental illness, drug/alcohol addiction and natural disasters. Whatever the reason is, we need to help homeless people and pray for them.

MEET ALEX

Alex, a young man from Romania slept on the streets in the U.K. because he couldn't find any work. He drank a lot of alcohol to numb how he felt. One night he was invited to sleep at a night shelter run by Christians. They helped him find some work and eventually a place to live. He was so touched by their love that he wanted to know more about God.

DID YOU KNOW?

The average age of death for a homeless person in the U.K. is just forty-seven years old!

PRAY

• For safety and protection of homeless people.

• That they would find hope in God.

WORLD CHANGERS About 100 million people throughout the world are completely homeless.

DAY 5: GREENLAND

Greenland is the world's largest island, but only a small number of people live there. It's a self-governing country under the Kingdom of Denmark and yet is found between the Arctic and Atlantic Oceans northeast of Canada. It was discovered by a Viking called Erik the Red who named it Greenland to attract more settlers. 'Whiteland', however, may be more accurate as about eighty-five percent of the country is covered in ice and snow! The average temperature only goes above freezing point for a few months in the summer! With snowcapped mountains and fjords, it's a beautiful country from which you can see the Northern Lights.

> "'...you have left the love you had in the beginning. So remember where you were before you fell. Change your hearts and do what you did at first.'"
> Revelation 2:4-5

Most people in Greenland are Inuit people who depend on fishing for a living. Towns are not connected by roads and so people have to travel by air or boat.

Christianity was introduced to Greenland by Erik's son, Leif Eriksson, over a thousand years ago and it became the first place in North America to have a church. Today there's a church building in most towns and many would say they are Christians, but sadly few have a personal relationship with Jesus. Modernization, unemployment, addiction to alcohol and living in a cold, isolated place can mean some Greenlanders feel very sad and lonely. God wants their hearts and lives to change as they find love and hope in him.

NEW WORDS: * Northern Lights: a display of coloured lights sometimes seen in the night sky in northern parts of the world. * Fjord: a long narrow inlet of the sea between high cliffs. * Arctic Circle: an imaginary line around the northern part of the world at about 66 degrees north of the equator.

PRAY

- For those feeling sad to find hope in Jesus.
- That the hearts of Greenlanders would change towards God.

FACT FILE:

Population: 56, 000   Capital: Nuuk

Main Religion: Christianity Official Language: Greenlandic [Kalaallisut]

DID YOU KNOW?

In the summer the sun never sets in Greenland. You can still see it in the middle of the night! It's called the 'midnight sun' and happens because Greenland is north of the Arctic Circle!

ON THE MAP

DAY 6: PERSECUTION

What is it like to be a Christian where you live? Can you go to church? Has anyone ever hurt you or put you in prison because you believe in Jesus? This is rare for most of us, but sadly for some Christians this is their way of life.

'Do not forget those who are in prison. Remember them as if you were in prison with them. Remember those who are suffering as if you were suffering with them.'
Hebrews 13:3

Today over 200 million Christians around the world are being persecuted for their faith. Persecuted means being treated in a cruel or unfair way and includes being beaten, put in prison or even put to death for simply following Jesus. Many risk their lives just to be able to worship God with others or read a Bible.

MEET HEE YOUNG

Hee Young's family was broken apart when North Korean authorities raided a secret meeting in her house. Her father disappeared and she never saw him again. Many other Christians were arrested at the same time and possibly sent to prison, a labour camp or even killed. Hee Young and the rest of her family were then forced to move to a remote area of North Korea and their Bible was taken away from them.

Let's support and stand with our persecuted family around the world, to let them know that they are not forgotten. Let's listen to their stories, speak up on their behalf, give money and pray for them.

DID YOU KNOW?

North Korea has been the most dangerous and difficult place in the world to live as a Christian since 2002!

PRAY

• For comfort, strength and protection of Christians who are being persecuted for their faith.

• For governments to make laws so that Christians are treated more fairly.

GET INTO IT!

Open Doors
60 years of serving persecuted Christians

Encourage Christians who are being persecuted by writing them a letter. Find out how you can do this by looking at the Open Doors website http://opendoorsuk.org/resources/letter/.

DAY 7: EGYPT

Egypt is in North Africa and is also part of the Middle East. It is mostly desert and so is a very hot, dry country. In Cairo, Egypt's capital city, only about 2.5 cm (1 inch) of rain falls per year! Most Egyptians live on a narrow strip of land along the River Nile as this is the only land that can be farmed. Tourists often visit Egypt to see the amazing huge pyramids that were built thousands of years ago as burial places for Egyptian kings called Pharaohs.

> "'I will call my people and gather them together. I will save them. And there will be as many of them as there used to be.'"
> Zechariah 10:8

We can read about Egypt in the Bible. It was the land where God used Jacob's son Joseph to save his family, where Moses was born and grew up, and a place of refuge for Jesus as a baby. Egyptians heard about Jesus on the Day of Pentecost in Jerusalem and it's thought that afterwards the Apostle Mark also went to share the good news with them. The Egyptian church grew and it became one of the first countries to welcome Christianity. Sadly, over the years since then, Egypt gradually changed to become a Muslim country where Christians were then persecuted. The church never completely disappeared, however, and although there are not as many Christians as there used to be, it's still the largest body of Christians in the Middle East. Today Egyptian Christians continue to be treated badly for their faith but, praise God, many remain strong.

DID YOU KNOW?

The Great Pyramid of Khufu at Giza is one of the largest pyramids ever built. Its base takes up as much space as about seven football pitches!

FACT FILE:

Population: 92 million

Capital: Cairo

Main Religion: Islam

Official Language: Arabic

PRAY

• There would be many Christians in Egypt like there used to be.

• For Christians to stand firm in their faith, even when they are persecuted.

ON THE MAP

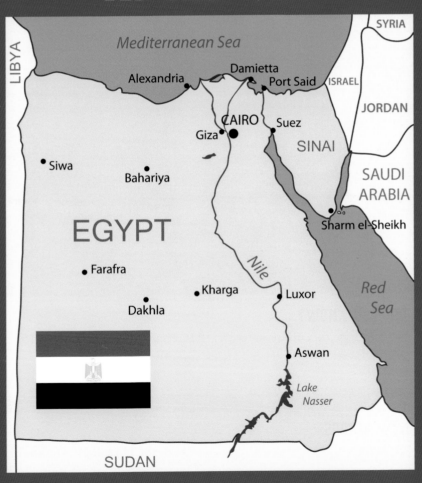

DAY 8: FLOODS

> 'He will help the needy when no one else will help them.'
> Psalm 72:12

A flood is a large amount of water covering an area of land that is normally dry. Floods are caused by extreme weather conditions such as very heavy rain and hurricanes, as well as by rivers overflowing, dams breaking or tsunamis. Some floods can develop slowly over days, but some can build up in just a few minutes when there's a lot of heavy rain. These are called flash floods.

Flooding is one of the most common natural disasters on Earth and is very expensive. People can lose their homes and all their belongings, and can be left without food or clean water. Buildings, roads, bridges and even whole towns can be damaged and crops can be destroyed. People can lose their lives drowning or from diseases from stagnant water.

Some tropical countries such as Bangladesh, India and Pakistan suffer flooding regularly. In 2010 Pakistan experienced one of its worst floods ever, with over one fifth of their country covered in water for months. Millions lost their homes and almost 2,000 people died. Nine-year-old Soni and her family survived the flood by living on the roof of their house for two weeks. She said, 'We lost everything. Our house, our village, our animals. We now have nothing left.'

DID YOU KNOW?

Just two feet [60 cm] of water can float a bus and just six inches [15 cm] of fast flowing water can knock you off your feet!

NEW WORDS:

* Tsunami: an enormous sea wave caused by an underwater earthquake or volcanic eruption which can cause a lot of destruction when it reaches land. * Stagnant water: water that is not flowing or moving.

PRAY

- For people affected by floods to experience God's comfort.

- For Christian organisations who help them.

- For protection from diseases caused by floods.

WORLD CHANGERS People can lose their homes and all their belongings when it floods.

DAY 9: MALDIVES

Maldives is a little country with a small population and so some people may never have heard of it. It is a group of small coral islands in the Indian Ocean, 370 miles (600 km) south-west of Sri Lanka. There are about 1,200 islands, but people only live on about 200 of them. Maldives is a place where some people go on holiday to enjoy its beautiful coral islands with white sandy beaches or go diving in its clear blue sea.

> "'Is anything too hard for the Lord? No!'"
> Genesis 18:14

It looks like paradise on the outside because of how pretty it is, but on the inside it has many difficulties. Crime and drugs are starting to become a problem and many Maldivians who work as fishermen are very poor. Also, Maldives is the lowest and flattest country in the world with most of it at about only one and a half metres above sea level. Maldivians are, therefore, worried that rising sea levels could mean their islands flood in the future.

Maldives is a country that boasts it is 100 percent Muslim. It doesn't allow anyone to openly follow any other religion. There are a few hundred Christians, but they have to meet in secret because if they were found out they may be put in prison. It's hard for Maldivians to hear about Jesus, but praise God nothing is too hard for him.

PRAY

- For protection and courage for Christian Maldivians who are being persecuted.
- For Maldivians to hear about Jesus.

FACT FILE:

Population: 364, 000   Capital: Malé

Main Religion: Islam   Official Language: Maldivian [Dhivehi]

ON THE MAP

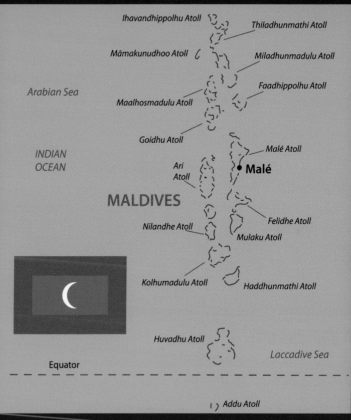

DAY 10: AVIATION MINISTRY

Aviation ministry means using planes to reach and help the world's most isolated people. Small planes go to places where there are no roads or where it's too dangerous and time-consuming to reach. God's love is shown by bringing help, hope and healing to the people living there. The pilots fly onto desert and jungle airstrips, lakes and rivers, tracks and roads to give practical help, share God's Word and help the sick.

'Neither height nor depth, nor anything else in all creation, will be able to separate us from the love of God that is in Christ Jesus our Lord.'
Romans 8:39 NIV

Whether it's bringing the gospel to the nomadic Maasai tribe in Tanzania, delivering boxes of presents to some of South Africa's poorest children or taking food to Aboriginal Australians in Arnhem Land, the planes are really important. Aviation ministry supports local pastors, missionaries and translators working in remote areas and provides training to locals. When people are sick, the planes save many lives by flying in medical help or flying out people who need to go to a hospital.

MEET LONA

Lona, a girl in Papua New Guinea, used to walk nine miles down a mountain every day to get drinking water for her village. One day she fell and broke her leg. Because there are no roads where she lives, she had to suffer the pain for four months. MAF [Mission Aviation Fellowship] heard about her from someone in a nearby village and so flew her to hospital to receive the treatment she needed.

DID YOU KNOW?

With over 135 aircraft working in about twenty-six countries, today, every four minutes, an MAF plane is taking off or landing somewhere in the world!

PRAY

• For the safety of pilots as they land on remote airstrips and rivers.

• For people in remote areas around the world to receive help, hope and healing through Jesus.

GET INTO IT!

Make a paper aeroplane, write a prayer on it and then throw it in the air while praying for missionary pilots and the people they are trying to help. Or read a book about a pilot such as Nate Saint in *Operation Auca* and learn what he gave up to serve God.

DAY 11: SOUTH KOREA

South Korea is situated in the southern part of the Korean Peninsula in East Asia. It's often known for the LG televisions, Hyundai cars and Samsung phones that it makes and sells to other countries. It used to be one country with North Korea, but in 1945 after World War II they were divided and in 1948 became two separate countries. South Korea is very different to North Korea. In North Korea there are not many Christians and it's the hardest country in the world to live as a Christian. In South Korea, however, many people have become Christians over the last sixty years. Praise God, almost a third of the country is now Christian and it has almost become the country's main religion.

'Early the next morning, Jesus woke and left the house while it was still dark. He went to a place to be alone and pray.'
Mark 1:35

PRAYER CONCERTS

Although with the growth of Christianity South Korea has some very large churches with thousands of members, it is the commitment to prayer by many Korean Christians that is a big example to us all. There are early morning and evening prayer meetings every day and all night, as well as weekend prayer concerts. It has also become one of the countries that send the largest number of missionaries to share about Jesus with people in other nations.

FACT FILE:
Population: 50 million

Main Religion: Non-religious

Capital: Seoul

Official Language: Korean

NEW WORD:
* Peninsula: an area of land surrounded by water on three sides.

PRAY

- Thank God for South Korea's commitment to prayer and mission.

- That the church in South Korea would not stop growing.

ON THE MAP

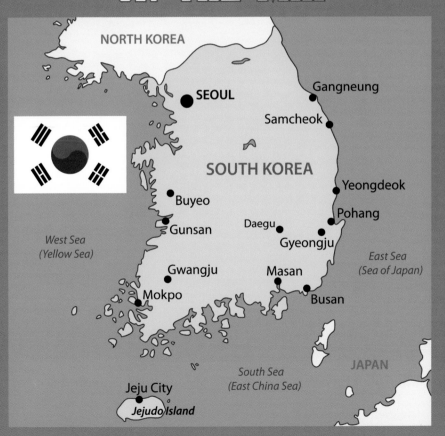

DAY 12: CHILD TRAFFICKING

Child trafficking is when children are moved within their country or abroad and forced to work in situations that are harmful to them. Many of them have no way of escape. Trafficking is modern-day slavery and has become the fastest growing crime worldwide. Every thirty seconds a child is trafficked. Child trafficking shatters the lives of over a million children and their families every year, but there are ways to stop it.

> "'Don't think these little children are worth nothing. I tell you that they have angels in heaven who are always with my Father in heaven.'"
> Matthew 18:10

MEET NAZEEB

Nazeeb was fourteen when men knocked on his door and offered him a good job in another city in India. His poor family needed the money, but he said, 'It turned out to be a terrible trap. I had to work for twenty-one hours each day—can you imagine it? It was so tiring and it was hard. The man had promised me money, but he didn't even give me one penny, so I couldn't help my family after all. I was far away from home. I was working with eleven other people and we were all locked in the factory. We had become slaves.'

Nazeeb managed to leave when he became too ill to work. Christians helped his family set up a chicken farm as a different way for him to earn money.

God doesn't want Nazeeb and other children to be slaves. Organisations like Tearfund are working to stop child trafficking by helping poor families at risk through a campaign called 'No Child Taken'.

DID YOU KNOW?

Children can be sold for as little as £10! ($13)

PRAY

• For the safety of children who are trafficked and for them to find a way of escape.

• For Christian organisations who are working to bring an end to child trafficking.

DAY 13: SAUDI ARABIA

Saudi Arabia is a large Arab country in the Middle East and occupies most of the Arabian Peninsula. It's the place to visit if you want to go to a camel market, watch camel racing or even try sandboarding. Saudi Arabia is one of the driest countries in the world with about ninety-five percent of the land covered in desert. It produces a lot of oil which it sells abroad, making it a rich country.

"'But I want you to know that the Son of Man has authority on earth to forgive sins.'"
Matthew 9:6 NIV

Saudi Arabia is the place where Islam, the world's second largest religion, started. The city of Mecca, in Saudi Arabia, is a special city for Muslims as Muhammad, the prophet of Islam, was born there. Every year there's an important event for Muslims called Hajj when about two million people from all over the world meet in Mecca. Also, Muslims around the world pray in the direction of Mecca five times a day. Islam teaches that Jesus is a prophet, but not that he is the Son of God, or that through him our sins can be forgiven. Let's pray that many Muslims would come to know the real Jesus.

Christians can live in Saudi Arabia but can't meet together or share their faith. Saudis from Muslim backgrounds who have become Christians face death if they are discovered. Even so, some still turn to Jesus and follow him – praise God.

DID YOU KNOW?

Saudi Arabians love eating baby camel meat and now some fast food restaurants offer baby camel burgers!

FACT FILE:

Population: 32 million
Main Religion: Islam
Capital: Riyadh

Official Language: Arabic

NEW WORD:

* Arab: a member of any Arabic-speaking people.

PRAY

• For the many Muslims in Saudi Arabia to come to know Jesus.

• For protection of secret believers.

• For a miracle to take place and Christianity to be allowed in Saudi Arabia.

ON THE MAP

DAY 14: CREATION CARE

God created the wonderful world that we live in. When we look at the beautiful trees, flowers, mountains, seas and animals all around us, we are reminded of God.

> 'In the beginning God created the sky and the earth... God looked at everything he had made, and it was very good.'
> Genesis 1: 1 & 31

We need to care for the world as it provides us with the oxygen, water, food, warmth and shelter that we need. If we pollute air, water and soil by making them dirty, it may cause extreme weather conditions such as droughts and floods, harm animals or even cause people to be unwell or die. Also, we should be careful not to waste the earth's resources such as wood, water and fuel or to use more of them than we need.

Unfortunately, we haven't always looked after God's creation well, but the good news is that we can change this by all helping and following the three Rs!

Reduce: Use less electricity and petrol by turning off lights when we don't need them and walking or cycling instead of using the car.

Reuse: Use things more than once, for example by using a plastic container for our lunch and cloth bags for our shopping.

Recycle: Make less rubbish by sending things such as glass bottles and cans to be recycled into something new.

DID YOU KNOW?

An aluminium can takes up to 500 years to break down but is recycled in six weeks! Recycling the can rather than making a new one saves enough electricity to power a TV for three hours!

PRAY

- That everyone would take better care of the world.
- That people would see the glory of God in creation.

GET INTO IT!

How many of these have you done this week?

1. Walked to school
2. Had a shower rather than a bath
3. Drawn or written on both sides of a piece of paper
4. Thrown rubbish in bins rather than dropping litter
5. Put leftover food and peelings on a compost heap

Well done if you have done three or more!

NEW WORDS:

* Pollute: to make [land, water, air, etc.] dirty and not safe or suitable to use.
* Drought: a long period of time during which there is very little or no rain.

DAY 15: COLOMBIA

Colombia is a country in the north-west of South America which got its name from the famous explorer Christopher Columbus. Its capital city Bogotá, which is in the Andes Mountain range, is one of the highest capital cities in the world. As well as mountains, Colombia also has rainforests, plains and beaches on both the North Pacific Ocean and the Caribbean Sea. The country has made money from oil, coffee and gold, and yet many Colombians are very poor. Large numbers live in slums and many children work on the streets.

"'Those who work to bring peace are happy. God will call them his sons.'"
Matthew 5:9

Colombia's history has sadly been filled with civil wars and violence. Although the violence is now decreasing, it still affects Colombians, with drugs sometimes being the cause of murders and kidnappings. Praise God, despite these problems, many are turning to Jesus and the church continues to grow.

FACT FILE:

Population: 48 million

Capital: Bogotá

Main Religion: Christianity

Official Language: Spanish

DID YOU KNOW?

Colombians like to drink hot chocolate with cheese dipped in it!

NEW WORD:

* Civil war: when groups of people within a country fight each other.

MEET JUAN

Juan is a ten-year-old boy who lives in a poor slum area of Bogotá with his mother and five brothers and sisters. His mum works long hours in a coffee factory and his dad is in prison. Juan's family are very poor and instead of going to school, Juan has to work unloading food from trucks. Life is hard for families like Juan's who live in slums with very little money.

PRAY

• That violence and the drug trade would end and Columbia would become a peaceful place to live.

• For help and hope for poor families living in slums.

ON THE MAP

DAY 16: CITIES

Today over half of the world's population live in cities. All over the world more people are moving to cities from rural areas, often because of work. Cities are therefore getting bigger, especially those in poorer countries.

'He saw the crowds of people and felt sorry for them because they were worried and helpless. They were like sheep without a shepherd.'
Matthew 9:36

Megacities are very large cities with a population of over ten million. Tokyo is a megacity in Japan where almost thirty-eight million people live. It's one of the most populated cities in the world along with Delhi in India and Shanghai in China.

Cities can be fun, exciting places to live, but they can also have many problems such as crime, air pollution, homelessness, too much traffic and poor housing.

God loves cities as he loves people and cities are filled with lots of different people. Some have moved there from different places and countries and

DID YOU KNOW?

Part of the job for workers in some of Tokyo's busy railway stations is to be a 'pusher'! They literally push people into crowded trains during rush hour!

NEW WORDS:

* Rural area: an area outside of cities and towns also called the countryside. * Rush hour: the busy time of day when large numbers of people are travelling to or returning from work.

there's often a mixture of young and old, rich and poor. They are places of opportunity to share about Jesus with many who have never heard the gospel before.

The Apostle Paul, in the Bible, planted churches in cities. This was not because people in rural areas were not so important, but because cities influenced surrounding areas which helped the gospel to spread. We also read in the Bible that God didn't let Jonah run away from the needs of the city of Nineveh. We shouldn't run away from the needs of cities either. We need to pray for cities throughout the world and tell people living in them about Jesus.

PRAY

• For a city, capital city or megacity in your country or somewhere in the world.

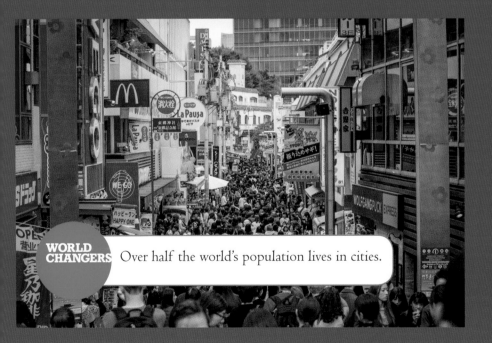

WORLD CHANGERS Over half the world's population lives in cities.

DAY 17: BRAZIL

Brazil is the largest country in the continent of South America and the largest Portuguese-speaking country in the world. It's known for its football, colourful carnivals and coffee. The famous Amazon River and a large part of the Amazon Rainforest are located in Brazil. These are home to millions of different types of animals and plants and the forest provides us with about twenty percent of the world's oxygen.

> 'First, I tell you to pray for all people. Ask God for the things people need, and be thankful to him.'
> I Timothy 2:I

There's much to thank God for in Brazil. There has been a huge increase in the number of evangelical Christians to about a quarter of the population. Big Christian events such as March for Jesus have given opportunity for Christians to celebrate their faith and tell people about Jesus. Brazil also sends out many missionaries to other countries to share about Jesus.

There are, however, still many needs in Brazil. Some of the numerous people groups including indigenous people have not yet been reached with the gospel. Tens of millions of people are very poor, and over eleven million live in slum areas called 'favelas'. Violent crime is a big problem and is often linked to drugs. There are also a large number of children who have to live or work on the streets.

DID YOU KNOW?

Brazil has won the World Cup football tournament five times, which is more than any other country!

FACT FILE:

Population: 208 million

Capital: Brasilia

Main Religion: Christianity

Official Language: Portuguese

PRAY

- Thank God for the many Christians in Brazil.
- For the gospel to reach all the different people groups.
- For poor people to be helped and find hope in God.

NEW WORDS:

* Evangelical Christians: Christians who take the Bible seriously and believe in Jesus Christ as their Saviour and Lord. * People group: a group of people with similar history, beliefs or even language. * Indigenous people: people who belong to the country where they are living, rather than coming there from another country.

ON THE MAP

DAY 18: HIV/AIDS

There is a virus that affects millions of people around the world. It weakens the body so it then struggles to fight germs. This virus is called HIV. AIDS is the final stage of HIV when you can no longer defend yourself against infections and diseases and so then get very sick and can die.

> 'My children, our love should not be only words and talk. Our love must be true love. And we should show that love by what we do.'
> I John 3:18

There are about thirty-six million people throughout the world living with HIV. It's worst in sub-Saharan Africa where in countries such as Swaziland and Botswana about one in five adults have the virus. Since the virus was first identified, around thirty-five million people have died of it. It has destroyed families and left millions of children without parents.

It is good, however, that the number of new people getting HIV has decreased. There's no cure for HIV, but there is medicine which strengthens the body and allows people to live a long and healthy life. Sadly, however, there are some people who can't afford the medicine or don't get the help and support they need.

We need to reach out and show God's love and care to people who have HIV as well as teach people how they can try to stop the spread of it.

DID YOU KNOW?

Our bodies are made up of trillions of cells! HIV attacks T cells which are a type of white blood cell that fight germs!

MEET LINLEY

Linley is a woman in Malawi who has HIV. Her husband died of AIDS four years ago. Linley now has to care for her three young children by herself. She feels fortunate compared to others as she receives medicine, food and clothes from a local Christian charity.

PRAY

• For healing and hope for people with HIV/AIDS.

• For more people to receive the medicine and help they need.

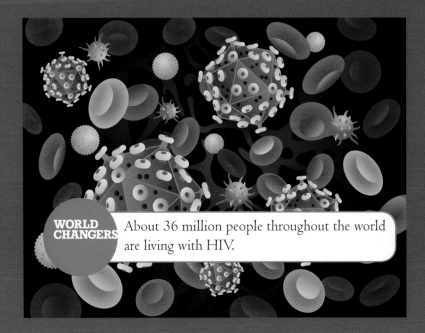

WORLD CHANGERS About 36 million people throughout the world are living with HIV.

NEW WORDS:

* HIV: Human Immunodeficiency Virus * AIDS: Acquired Immunodeficiency Syndrome

DAY 19: FRANCE

France is the third largest country in Europe and is known for its gorgeous coasts and beaches, old castles and châteaux as well as historic cities and villages. It is famous for the wine it produces, its delicious cheeses, famous painters and even Disneyland! More tourists visit France than any other country worldwide. They visit places such as the Alps and Pyrenees Mountains and the Eiffel Tower in Paris.

'Trust the Lord with all your heart. Don't depend on your own understanding.'
Proverbs 3:5

Although France is one of the richest and most beautiful countries in the world and has a Christian history, sadly many have turned away from God. A large number of French people now don't believe in God at all and don't know what a friend Jesus can be. Instead of relying on God, they rely on themselves and on their own understanding of life. Also, there aren't many evangelical churches in towns and villages, and those places that do have them often don't have a pastor.

Over the years, many people have come to live in France from places such as Africa and other countries in Europe. Some of these people are Christians who are strengthening the French church. However, some are Muslims who have little opportunity to hear the gospel.

DID YOU KNOW?

The Tour de France is the most famous bicycle race in the world. It takes place in France every year. It covers around 3,500 km [2,175 miles] in twenty-three days!

FACT FILE:

Population: 64 million

Capital: Paris

Main Religion: Christianity

Official Language: French

PRAY

• For French people to trust in God and not depend on their own understanding.

• For people to share about Jesus with Muslims living in France.

NEW WORD:

* Châteaux: large French country houses or castles.

ON THE MAP

DAY 20: HUNGER

There is enough food in the world to feed everyone and yet about one in nine people go hungry every day. This means that they don't have enough food to give them the energy they need. Hunger often stops people from being able to work, play or study. It can weaken their bodies so that they can't fight diseases and then they can become ill or die.

*""""I was hungry, and you gave me food. I was thirsty, and you gave me something to drink...
I tell you the truth. Anything you did for any of my people here, you also did for me.""""*
Matthew 25: 35 & 40

Most people who are hungry live in the continents of Asia and Africa. People are often hungry because they are too poor to be able to buy or grow enough food, but war, famine, weather and natural disasters also cause hunger. Hunger is one of the biggest risks to health in the world and yet it's completely solvable.

MEET HASSAN

When we have enough food to eat in our cupboards, it's hard to imagine what life is like for those who always feel hungry, like nine-year-old Hassan in Somalia. His family have little money and their crops have died because there wasn't enough rain. Hassan wakes up hungry every morning and doesn't know when he will get his next meal.

DID YOU KNOW?

One third of food produced is never eaten and therefore wasted! How can we stop this from happening?

PRAY

• For money to help feed hungry people.

• For organisations who distribute food to those who need it.

• That when the need for food has been met, people would also have a hunger to know God.

NEW WORD:

* Famine: a severe shortage of food.

WORLD CHANGERS About one in nine people go hungry every day.

THE
WORLD

AFRICA

EUROPE

DAY 21: SOUTH AFRICA

South Africa covers the southern part of the continent of Africa. It's often called the 'rainbow nation' because of its many languages, races and cultures. It has eleven official languages. Most people speak at least two to three, one of which is usually English or Afrikaans.

'Finally, all of you should live together in peace. Try to understand each other. Love each other as brothers. Be kind and humble.'
I Peter 3:8

Praise God that a large number of South Africans are Christians. Some are involved in Christian work helping people or telling people about Jesus in South Africa or abroad. South Africa was also the country that started the Global Day of Prayer which has influenced the world.

Sadly, however, South Africa has a history of 'apartheid'. This meant that the majority of the country who were not white people were treated unfairly and were forced to live in separate areas from whites. This was challenged by people including a famous man, called Nelson Mandela, who eventually became the president of the country. Fortunately apartheid has now ended, but it still affects the country with people feeling mistrust, fear and hurt.

South Africa also has problems with violence, crime and HIV/AIDS. Many poor people live in slum areas called townships where there are terrible living conditions and they struggle to find work.

FACT FILE:

Population: 54 million

Capitals: Pretoria, Cape Town, Bloemfontein

Main Religion: Christianity

Official Languages: 11 different languages

NEW WORD:

* Culture: the beliefs, behaviour and way of life of a group of people.

PRAY

- That the church would be an example by loving people regardless of language, race or culture.
- For forgiveness and healing from apartheid.
- For the poor living in the townships to receive help and hope in Jesus.

DID YOU KNOW?

A small antelope called the Springbok is the national animal of South Africa and is one of the fastest land animals in the world! It can reach speeds up to 90 km/hr [56 mph]!

ON THE MAP

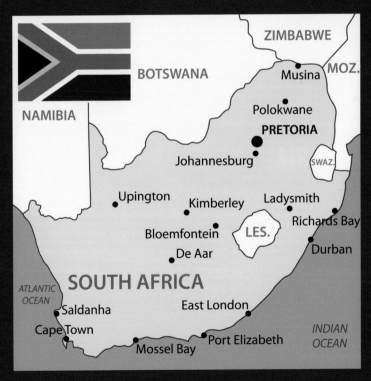

DAY 22: ORPHANS

An orphan is a child whose parents have died and so they don't have a parent to look after them anymore. This is rare in most countries but unfortunately war, famine, diseases and natural disasters such as floods and earthquakes have created millions of orphans in the world, especially in Asia, Africa and Latin America.

'Religion that God accepts is this: caring for orphans or widows who need help.'
James 1:27

Without the care of parents, orphans face a difficult life. Some are fortunate and are cared for by their extended families such as aunts, uncles or grandparents, or are even adopted. Some live in orphanages, but sadly there are many who have no one to turn to. They often end up living on the streets, having to work and to find food to survive.

In the Bible, God tells us to care for orphans and protect them. We can do this by praying for them, giving money towards their care or even adopting them ourselves.

MEET GLORIA

Gloria was born in Liberia in June 2014. Sadly, both her parents died of a disease called Ebola. No one wanted to look after Gloria and her brothers and sisters because even though they were well, people were scared they could catch Ebola from them. Praise God a Christian lady called Justina took in the children. They are now settling into life as a new family with the support of a local Tearfund project who are helping them with money for food and school fees.

PRAY

• For orphans to be safe and have hope in Jesus.

• That they would have someone to care for them and know God as their Father.

DID YOU KNOW?

J.R.R. Tolkien, who wrote *The Hobbit* and *The Lord of the Rings*, and Johann Sebastian Bach, the famous composer, were both orphans!

WORLD CHANGERS

The Bible tells us to care for orphans.

DAY 23: THE GAMBIA

The Gambia is a little, narrow West African country. It's surrounded by Senegal and has a small coast on the Atlantic Ocean which attracts many tourists. It is the smallest country in mainland Africa and the Gambia River flows through the middle of it. It's also one of the poorest countries in the world with most Gambians working as farmers.

> "'Here I am! I stand at the door and knock. If anyone hears my voice and opens the door, I will come in and eat with him. And he will eat with me.'"
> Revelation 3:20

The Gambia is a Muslim country with only a small number of Christians. Unlike some other Muslim African countries however, there's more freedom to share about Jesus.

The country is a mix of thirty different people groups. The largest is the Mandinka followed by the Fulani, Wolof and Jola. Many of these people groups have never heard about Jesus.

MEET BAKARY

A man called Bakary who is a member of the Jola people group was nearly blind and although he saw healers and mediums, no one could help. A missionary employed him as a language teacher and took him to church where he became one of the first Jola Christians in Sibanor. Years later he had an operation which allowed him to see again. He then helped with the translation of the Jola New Testament and is now working on the Old Testament.

DID YOU KNOW?

The Gambia is the only country in the world where people use marbles to vote in elections! They drop a marble into a hole marked by the politician they choose!

God is knocking at the door of the hearts of Gambian people. Let's pray they will hear his voice as Bakary did and invite him into their lives.

PRAY

• For continued freedom to spread the gospel in The Gambia.

• For Muslims from all the different people groups to hear about Jesus.

ON THE MAP

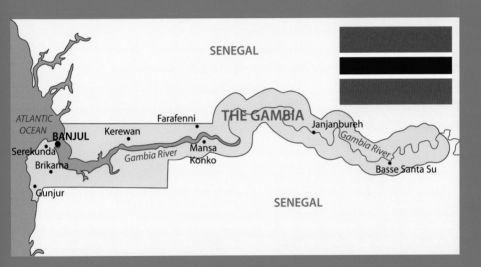

FACT FILE:

Population: 2 million
Main Religion: Islam
Capital: Banjul
Official Language: English

NEW WORDS:

* Healer: a person who believes they are able to cure the sick, using special powers.
* Medium: a person who claims to be able to communicate with the spirits of dead people.

DAY 24: JUDAISM

Judaism is the religion of Jewish people who number about fourteen million. They live throughout the world but especially in Israel and the United States.

'The woman said, "I know that the Messiah is coming." (Messiah is the One called Christ). "When the Messiah comes, he will explain everything to us." Then Jesus said, "He is talking to you now. I am he."'
John 4:25-26

Jews worship God who created the universe and some of them believe that God will one day send a Messiah. There are some Jews who have recognised Jesus as the Messiah and have become Christians. Most Jews however don't believe the Messiah was Jesus. They believe Jesus was only a Jewish teacher and not the Son of God. They therefore don't have a personal faith in Jesus, and continue to be guided only by the laws and customs found in the first five books of the Bible called the Torah.

Some Jews follow the laws more strictly than others, for example covering their heads with a kippah [skullcap] and not cutting their beards or sidelocks. Jews worship God in synagogues on Friday evenings and Saturdays, and their spiritual leaders are called Rabbis. They are proud that they are often called God's chosen people in the Old Testament, and have a lot of festivals during the year to remind them of their history.

Israel has always been a very special place for Jews. Most of them had to leave it many years ago and went to live in other countries where sometimes they were treated badly or killed, especially during World War II.

DID YOU KNOW?

The Vulcan Salute, used by Mr Spock on Star Trek, was taken from the priestly blessing of Judaism!

PRAY

- For Jewish people to believe and love Jesus as their Messiah and the Son of God.

WORLD CHANGERS Some Jewish boys cover their heads with a kippah and don't cut their sidelocks.

DAY 25: BHUTAN

Bhutan is a tiny country between China and India in the eastern Himalaya Mountains. Its violent thunderstorms have meant that it's often nicknamed the 'Land of the Thunder Dragon'. Bhutan has been an isolated country for many years, not just because it's among the highest mountains in the world, but also to protect its culture from outside influence. Today it's less isolated; tourists can now visit the country, and television and Internet are allowed. Bhutanese culture is still, however, very strong in everyday life. Its national costume is worn by government workers and in schools as well as on special occasions. Men wear a knee-length robe called a Gho and women wear an ankle-length dress called a Kira.

'Finally, be strong in the Lord and in his great power.' Ephesians 6:10

Some people in Bhutan are Hindus, but most are Buddhists. Buddhism is not just a religion but also a way of life in Bhutan. It has a lot of influence and all around the country you can see prayer flags, temples and red-robed monks.

Bhutan is one of the least evangelised countries in the world. There are not many Christians and many have never heard about Jesus. When someone in Bhutan becomes a Christian they are sometimes rejected by their family and community. They may face pressure to return to Buddhism and be treated badly for their faith, especially for sharing about Jesus with other people. Despite this, the church is slowly growing and most believers are standing strong in their faith.

FACT FILE:

Population: 775,000

Main Religion: Buddhism

Capital: Thimphu

Official Language: Dzongkha

NEW WORD:

* Buddhist: someone who believes in Buddhism, a religion that started in Asia and follows the teachings of Buddha.

PRAY

- For more people in Bhutan to follow Jesus.

- For continued strength for Christians in the country.

DID YOU KNOW?

Bhutan's national sport is a form of archery in which teams face each other across a field and fire sharp arrows at a target opposite. They try to distract their opponents by waving their arms and making fun of them!

ON THE MAP

DAY 26: ADDICTIONS

Unfortunately some people find themselves addicted to things like drugs and alcohol for various reasons. This can cause a lot of problems in their lives. They find themselves doing things that they wouldn't normally do and can lose their jobs, money and sometimes their family and friends. Addictions ruin their lives, but the good news is that God can set them free and give them a new life.

> "'If you continue to obey my teaching, you are truly my followers. Then you will know the truth. And the truth will make you free... So if the Son makes you free, then you will be truly free.'"
> John 8: 31, 32 & 36

MEET STEVE

Steve started taking drugs when he was a teenager, after his dad left home. He became addicted to them and his life was terrible. He even ended up in prison for a while. Steve wanted to change but didn't know how and couldn't break free

THEN   NOW

of his addiction. Eventually some Christian friends told him that Jesus could heal him. They recommended a Christian centre for people with addictions called Betel. Steve went to the centre and although it was difficult at first, he soon began to live a different way. He now says, 'Today, I live in the knowledge that God has set me free, from both my addictions and my old ways of thinking. As the Bible promises, I've been changed…my mind's been renewed.'

Steve is now married to Maria and together they are serving the Lord with Betel helping other people with addictions. They are blessed with a baby boy called John-Joseph.

PRAY

• That people would be set free from addictions and lead new lives in God.

• For Christian centres who reach out to those who have addictions.

DID YOU KNOW?

Harmful use of alcohol caused 3.3 million deaths around the world in 2012!

NEW WORD:

* Addicted: to be dependent on or really want something even if it can harm your health.

DAY 27: AFGHANISTAN

Afghanistan is a dry and mountainous country in South Asia. It has been on the news a lot because of all the fighting that has happened there. After many years of war it has become one of the poorest countries in the world. It's now trying to recover, but still faces violence and has landmines scattered throughout the country. War caused a lot of children to lose their parents, and some adults were injured and are now disabled. It's a dangerous place to live because of violence and lack of health care and clean water. Almost one in ten children die before they reach their fifth birthday, and of those who do survive many never go to school.

> "'If your faith is as big as a mustard seed, you can say to this mountain, 'Move from here to there'. And the mountain will move. All things will be possible for you.'"
> Matthew 17:20

Afghanistan is one of the most unreached countries in the world. It has many mosques but not a single church building. Although there have been reports that the number of Christians has been increasing, there still aren't many believers. Also, the few Afghans who are Christians are sometimes treated badly for their faith. It seems that the world has given up on it. However, God has not. Let's pray in faith that God would move in this country and that many Afghans would believe in Jesus.

DID YOU KNOW?

Buzkashi is the national sport of Afghanistan. Two teams try to move the body of a dead goat to a scoring area while riding on a horse!

FACT FILE:

Population: 33 million

Capital: Kabul

Main Religion: Islam

Official Languages: Pashtu and Dari

PRAY

- For peace and unity in Afghanistan.
- For courage and protection of Afghan believers.
- For God to move in the country with many becoming Christians.

NEW WORDS:

* Landmine: a bomb that is buried in the ground and explodes when someone steps on it or drives over it. * Unreached: a people group or country who have not yet been reached with the gospel. * Mosque: a Muslim place of worship.

ON THE MAP

DAY 28: HUI IN CHINA

The Hui [pronounced Hway] are a group of about thirteen million people who live across almost every part of China but particularly in the north-west. Hundreds of years ago Arab and Persian traders, soldiers and craftsmen travelled to China where they settled and became known as the Hui. They speak Chinese like anyone else; however, most Hui are Muslim. They are the largest Muslim group of people in China and so this is why Islam in China is sometimes called 'the Hui religion'. They worship in thousands of mosques throughout the country and are often known as 'Chinese Muslims'. Some Hui men wear white caps on their heads and Hui women wear head scarves.

'Jesus answered, "I am the way. And I am the truth and the life. The only way to the Father is through me."'
John 14:6

Most Hui haven't heard the good news about Jesus our Saviour and there are only a few churches among them. Praise God that despite this, he is working in the lives of Hui people.

THE WAY

A young Hui girl grew up believing that to be Hui is to be Muslim. She didn't fully understand Islam, but it was a way of life and she had never questioned it. When she went to college she heard some people talking about Jesus being the 'Way'. She had never heard about Jesus before and so started studying the Bible. She learnt more about Jesus and eventually gave her life to him.

PRAY

- For more people to share about Jesus with the Hui.

- For Hui people to know that Jesus is the only way, truth and life.

DID YOU KNOW?

Like Muslims all around the world, many Hui fast during the Muslim month of Ramadan. Men, women and children over about the age of twelve are expected to fast from sunrise to sunset! This means no food or drink all day!

WORLD CHANGERS Hui are the largest Muslim group of people in China.

DAY 29: NEW ZEALAND

New Zealand is made up of two main islands called the North Island and the South Island as well as many smaller ones. It's a remote country located about 1,600 km [1,000 miles] south-east of Australia. New Zealand is just slightly larger than the U.K. and yet only has a population of four and a half million people. New Zealanders are sometimes nicknamed Kiwis. A kiwi is a flightless bird that lives in New Zealand and is its national symbol.

'Then I heard the Lord's voice. He said, "Whom can I send? Who will go for us?" So I said, "Here I am. Send me!"'
Isaiah 6:8

The first people to live in New Zealand were the Maori people who travelled from the Pacific islands of Polynesia. Hundreds of years later, settlers from Europe arrived and fought with the Maori over land. The Maori named the country Aotearoa which means 'land of the long white cloud'. It's a beautiful country which you may have seen in *The Hobbit* or *The Lord of the Rings* movies which were filmed in New Zealand.

There are many Christians in New Zealand. Praise God that some of them have taken up the challenge to share about Jesus with those around them who say they have no religion, as well as with immigrants who also live there. Many New Zealand Christians have also gone to tell people about Jesus in different countries around the world.

FACT FILE:

Population: 4.5 million   Capital: Wellington

Main Religion: Christianity   Official Languages: English and Maori

PRAY

• Thank God for New Zealand Christians who share about Jesus with people living around them and in other countries.

• For those who say they have no religion to believe in Jesus.

DID YOU KNOW?

New Zealand once produced coins with images of Gandalf, Frodo and the Dragon Smaug from *The Hobbit* and *The Lord of the Rings*! They would be cool coins to collect!

ON THE MAP

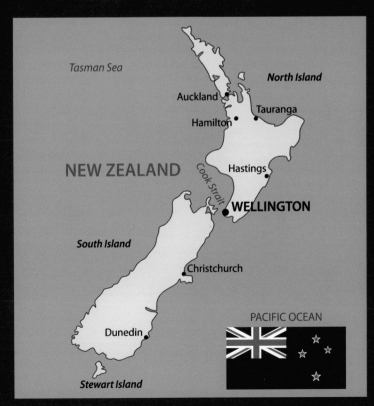

DAY 30: HINDUISM

Hinduism is the third largest world religion with about one billion Hindus worldwide. It's a religion or way of life that grew out of the way people lived and worshipped in India many years ago. Today it's the main religion in countries such as India and Nepal. Although Hindus believe there's only one god called Brahman, they say there are many ways to reach him and think about him. They therefore worship gods and goddesses as different forms of that god. At temples or shrines in their homes, they pray and offer flowers, food and incense to these gods.

'There is only one God. And there is only one way that people can reach God. That way is through Jesus Christ, who is also a man.'
I Timothy 2:5

Hindus also believe that when they die they will keep coming back to life again as another person, animal or plant. How they behave in this life, they believe that will affect their next life.

Every Hindu is born into a group called a caste which can affect a person's everyday life. Some castes are considered better than others, with the lower castes doing the jobs no one else wants to do.

MEET SHELY

Shely Ganguly was a Hindu from a high caste in India. Her family had a shrine in her home where they worshipped their many gods. Shely studied at university in the U.K. where she heard that Jesus was the only way to come to the one true, living God. She started going to church and then became a Christian.

DID YOU KNOW?

Hindus respect cows and so don't eat beef! This means no beef burgers!

PRAY

• That Hindus, like Shely, would discover Jesus to be the only way to God to receive forgiveness and eternal life.

NEW WORD:

* Hindu family shrine: a place in the home where the family worships a picture or statue of their favourite god.

WORLD CHANGERS Hinduism is the third largest world religion.

DAY 31: NEPAL

If you'd like to see the highest point in the world then Nepal is the place to visit. It's a country between China and India which contains a large part of the highest mountain range in the world called the Himalayas. With eight of the world's ten tallest mountains, it's a beautiful country showing the amazing work of God, the creator. Many tourists visit Nepal to look at its stunning scenery or to climb up mountains including Mount Everest which is the highest point on earth.

'The deepest places on earth are his. And the highest mountains belong to him… He created the land with his own hands. Come, let's bow down and worship him.'
Psalm 95: 4-6

Sadly, Nepal is one of the poorer countries in the world. Some children and young people don't have the opportunity to go to school, and child labour is also a big problem.

Over eighty percent of Nepali people are Hindus and if you're a Christian you can be treated badly. However, through prayer and the boldness of Nepali Christians in sharing the gospel, the number of Christians has hugely increased. Now there's a church in every one of the seventy-five districts of Nepal and in almost every people and caste group there are some believers.

DID YOU KNOW?

Nepal's flag is the only national flag that is not a square or rectangle! It's made up of two overlapping triangles which represent Nepal's Himalaya Mountains and its two main religions [Hinduism and Buddhism]!

FACT FILE:

Population: 29 million   Capital: Kathmandu

Main Religion: Hinduism   Official Language: Nepali

PRAY

• For the poor of Nepal, especially children and young people.

• Thank God for Nepali Christians who have told others about Jesus.

• For Jesus to be worshipped by even more Nepali people.

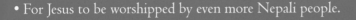

GET INTO IT!

William Carey first translated the New Testament into Nepali in 1821. You can read about him in the book, *Ten Boys Who Changed the World*.

ON THE MAP

DAY 32: EUROPE

Europe is the second smallest of seven continents in the world. It covers about four million square miles, which is just a little larger than the United States. Europe, however, is the third most populated continent and so is a crowded continent with about fifty different countries.

'Let us examine and look at what we have done. Then let us return to the Lord. Let us lift up our hands and pray from our hearts. Let us say to God in heaven, "We have sinned and turned against you."'
Lamentations 3:40-42

Sadly, although Europe used to be strongly Christian, it's now a continent where Christianity is declining. While in Africa and Asia churches are filling up, churches in Europe are closing their doors. Many Europeans no longer go to church or have a relationship with God. Europe, which once sent missionaries around the world, is now in deep need of them itself. William Tyndale was killed in Belgium about 500 years ago for translating the Bible into English so that ordinary people could read it, but now only around one percent of Belgians are evangelical Christians.

Europe has been the destination for many immigrants looking for a better future. Some of these are Christian and have brought encouragement to the church; however some are Muslim and have yet to hear about Jesus. They too need to be reached with the gospel.

DID YOU KNOW?

Europe is home to the smallest country in the world. The Vatican City has a tiny population of about 800 people and is only 0.17 square miles [0.44 square kilometres]! This is the size of an average golf course!

PRAY

• For Europeans to return to the Lord and worship him again.

• For the many young people in Europe who are growing up not hearing about Jesus.

• For Muslims in Europe to be reached with the gospel.

WORLD CHANGERS Europe is a crowded continent with about fifty different countries.

DAY 33: VIETNAM

Vietnam is a long, narrow country in South East Asia. Its shape is sometimes compared to the letter 's'. It's often known for the 'Vietnam War' which was fought between the north and south of the country and also involved some other nations. It lasted almost twenty years and many people died. In 1976, shortly after the end of the war, Vietnam became a communist country. It's one of only a few communist countries that still exist today. Communism means the state controls and owns many things, which can restrict people's freedom.

> "'You must choose for yourselves today. You must decide whom you will serve…As for me and my family, we will serve the Lord.'"
> Joshua 24:15

Many Vietnamese are Buddhist, but they also pray and make offerings of gifts to the spirits of their dead relatives. This is called ancestral worship. They believe the dead relatives can influence their lives for good or bad and so are often scared of them.

The law in Vietnam says people are free to follow whatever religion they choose, but unfortunately many Christians have suffered for their faith. Praise God that, despite this, the church has continued to grow.

DID YOU KNOW?

Snake wine is a Vietnamese drink made with rice wine and a pickled snake inside it! It's thought to cure any sickness!

FACT FILE:

Population: 93 million   Capital: Hanoi

Main Religion: Buddhism   Official Language: Vietnamese

MEET TRAN VAN VINH

Tran Van Vinh is a Christian leader in northern Vietnam. One day the local authorities came to his house and arrested him. They wanted him to turn away from his faith and lead people back to worshipping spirits. Thank God he did not!

PRAY

- For Vietnamese to turn from ancestral worship and follow Jesus.
- Thank God for the growing church in Vietnam.
- For continued strength and comfort of Vietnamese Christians who are treated badly for their faith.

ON THE MAP

75

DAY 34: ROMA PEOPLE

The Roma [or Romani] are an ethnic minority group of people who often travelled in caravans from place to place and had no permanent home. They are often known among English-speaking people as gypsies. It's believed Roma originated from India, however, most of them now live in Europe and the Americas. We don't know exactly how many Roma people there are, but it's estimated they number about ten million. They are one of the largest ethnic minority groups in Europe.

'Among them you shine like stars in the dark world.'
Philippians 2:15

Family and community are at the centre of Roma life, as well as the colourful music and dance they enjoy. They are also sometimes associated with horses, fortune-telling and large families. Because of Roma's distinct culture and values they have been misunderstood and treated badly over the years, which sadly still continues in some places today. Most have now chosen to live in permanent houses or in caravans in one place, but unfortunately some have been forced to do this by the country where they live.

Roma have been described as 'many stars scattered in the sight of God'. Praise God that over the last fifty years many Roma people have turned to God. Some have had visions, been healed and found new life in Jesus. Let's pray that they would shine like stars and reflect God's light to people around them who don't know Jesus.

DID YOU KNOW?

It's believed that Roma were probably called 'Gypsy' for the first time by Europeans who mistakenly thought they had come from Egypt!

PRAY

• Thank God for the many Roma people who have become Christians.

• That they would shine God's light to those around them.

NEW WORD:

* Ethnic minority: a group of people who have a different culture, language, religion or nationality to the majority of people where they live.

WORLD CHANGERS Roma are one of the largest ethnic minority groups in Europe.

DAY 35: SOMALIA

Somalia is a country on the eastern coastline of the continent of Africa. It's on an area of land called the Horn of Africa which juts out hundreds of kilometres into the Arabian Sea in the shape of a horn.

'Surely the Lord's power is enough to save you.'
Isaiah 59:1

Somalians have gone through a lot of suffering, especially over the last twenty years. Many years of civil war and fighting as well as drought have led to Somalia becoming one of the poorest countries in the world. It's now one of the hardest places on earth to be a child, with about one in seven Somali children dying before their fifth birthday.

Islam is the main religion in Somalia and its leaders say that there is no room for Christianity, Christians or churches in its country. It's the second most difficult country in the world to live as a Christian, and yet there are a small number of Christians who live there. They are hated and treated badly and so have to worship secretly in houses. It seems impossible for anyone to become a Christian in Somalia, but thankfully we know the Lord's power is enough to save.

One Somalian believer told a Christian radio station, 'I had been a conservative Muslim … but now I am a believer and that is because of your programme. I am no longer a Muslim because I received and accepted the gospel after I heard it from you.'

FACT FILE:

Population: 11 million

Capital: Mogadishu

Main Religion: Islam

Official Languages: Somali and Arabic

PRAY

• For an end to the years of fighting and drought.

• For strength for Somali Christians who suffer for their faith.

• For Christian radio to reach Somalians for Jesus.

DID YOU KNOW?

In 2010 Somali pirates were responsible for forty-four percent of sea piracy cases in the whole world!

ON THE MAP

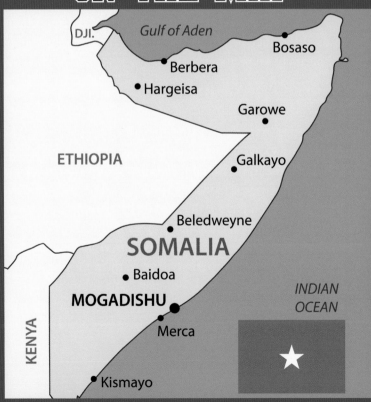

DAY 36: UNREACHED PEOPLE GROUPS

P eople groups are groups of people with similar history, beliefs or even language. Some countries have many different people groups, for example South Africa has sixty-five. There are about 195 countries in the world today but around 16,550 people groups. About 6,700 of them have little or no way to hear the good news about Jesus. We call them unreached because they are yet to be reached with the gospel.

> "'So go and make followers of all people in the world.'"
> Matthew 28:19

God wants all these unreached people groups to have the opportunity to hear about Jesus. He wants the Bugis in Indonesia, the Brahmin in India and the Hausa in Nigeria to know about him.

GONDS

The Gonds are another example of a large unreached people group. There are over fifteen million Gondi people found mainly in central India. They live in small villages close to rivers and forests and most of them work as farmers. Their main language is Gondi, but they can also speak other languages including Hindi. Most Gonds are influenced by Hinduism, but some also believe in ancestral worship and are animists. This means they believe there are spirits living in everything around them such as in trees and mountains. Gonds are afraid of these spirits and so offer sacrifices to them for protection, such as a goat that has been killed. They think although some spirits are nice, some are evil and make bad things happen. Gonds need to hear the good news that they don't have to be afraid of spirits, but sadly few have ever heard about Jesus.

PRAY

• That there would be more missionaries to unreached people groups.

• For Gonds to hear about Jesus and choose to follow him.

GET INTO IT!

Choose an unreached people group on the Joshua Project website https://joshuaproject.net/resources/prayer_cards. Read about them and see what they look like. Then print out the card and pray for them.

WORLD CHANGERS Gonds need to hear the good news about Jesus.

DID YOU KNOW?

The Jungle Book story was based in the area of India where Gond people live!

DAY 37: SRI LANKA

Sri Lanka is an island south of India which used to be called Ceylon. It's a country with beautiful beaches, stunning scenery and lots of elephants. Many Sri Lankans are farmers growing rice, tea, rubber and coconuts, but some work in factories making clothes which are sold around the world.

"'Also, the kingdom of heaven is like a man looking for fine pearls. One day he found a very valuable pearl. The man went and sold everything he had to buy that pearl.'"
Matthew 13:45-46

Rice and curry is the most common meal in Sri Lanka and is eaten with the fingertips of the right hand —with no cutlery!

The shape of Sri Lanka is sometimes compared to a teardrop. The country has gone through some very sad things with a civil war lasting many years ending in 2009, and a tsunami in 2004 which killed over 30,000 Sri Lankans. Sri Lanka, however, is also described as the 'Pearl of the Indian Ocean'. This is because it is pearl-shaped and pearls are found in the oceans surrounding it. Sri Lanka is a treasure like a pearl to God which he loves deeply.

Most Sri Lankans are Buddhists, but there are also Hindus, Muslims and a small number of Christians. Praise God that over the last fifty years Christianity has grown, even though it has met opposition and persecution. Let's pray that many more Sri Lankans would also find God to be their real treasure and become Christians.

FACT FILE:

Population: 21 million

Capital: Colombo

Main Religion: Buddhism

Official Languages: Sinhala and Tamil

PRAY

- For more Sri Lankans to come to know Jesus.

- For the many villages who have yet to hear about Jesus.

DID YOU KNOW?

Sri Lanka has one of the highest rates of death from snakebites in the world!

ON THE MAP

DAY 38: DIASPORA

Diaspora is a word used to describe the movement of people from their home country to other places in the world. India has the largest diaspora with sixteen million people from India living outside of their country. This is followed by twelve million from Mexico. In total there are about 244 million people living in countries other than where they were born, including twenty million refugees.

'Instead, they were longing for a better country - a heavenly one. Therefore God is not ashamed to be called their God, for he has prepared a city for them.'
Hebrews 11:16 NIV

Sometimes these people have moved for just a short period of time, for example to study at university in another country. Often it's for a long time or permanently. People move to another country for different reasons, including work or a better way of life. For others it may be to escape danger in their home country. These people are called refugees. For whatever reason though, these people need our friendship, love and help. Some of them are Christians and God is using them to share their faith in their new country. However, many have come from places where they may never have heard the gospel before. We have a wonderful opportunity to share about Jesus with them.

GET INTO IT!

Think of someone who lives near you or is at your school with you who has moved there from a different country. You could make friends with them, help them, invite them to church and pray for them.

MEET JOSEPH

Joseph, an eleven-year-old boy, got to know people living near him who had come from other countries. He invited his local Indian shop owner, Nepali restaurant workers, Iranian barber and Dutch neighbour to church especially to an International Friendship Evening held there. Some of them went; they got to know Christians and heard a little about the Christian faith.

PRAY

• That people who have moved to another country would know Jesus.

• That we would reach out to them with God's love.

DID YOU KNOW?

In 2015 about one in eight of the U.K. population had been born abroad, mainly in Poland, India and Pakistan!

WORLD CHANGERS Invite people to an International Friendship Evening at a church.

DAY 39: INDONESIA

Indonesia is a country in the continent of Asia that is made up of about 17, 500 islands scattered on either side of the equator. Imagine living in a country that's not just one piece of land but so many islands. Indonesia is the fourth most populated country in the world after China, India and the U.S.A. The island of Java where many Indonesians live is the world's most populated island.

'People in the islands of the sea, praise the name of the Lord, the God of Israel.'
Isaiah 24:15

Indonesia has almost 780 different people groups and over 700 languages are spoken there. From a faith point of view it can appear confusing because it has the largest Muslim population in the world and yet has the second largest number of Christians in South East Asia. Many people groups in Indonesia have never heard about Jesus and yet there are many large churches and in the capital of Jakarta some churches have thousands of members! Some strict Muslims, however, want Indonesia to be a completely Muslim country and so Christians sometimes face opposition and can be treated badly for believing in Jesus.

DID YOU KNOW?

Indonesia is home to some of the rarest animals in the world, such as fish that climb trees to catch insects and spiders that catch and eat small birds in giant webs!

FACT FILE:

Population: 258 million   Capital: Jakarta

Main Religion: Islam   Official Language: Indonesian

PRAY

• For Christians on every island to share about Jesus, especially to unreached people groups.

• For strength for Christians in Indonesia who are treated badly for believing in Jesus.

NEW WORD:

* Equator: an imaginary circle around the earth, an equal distance from the North and South Poles.

ON THE MAP

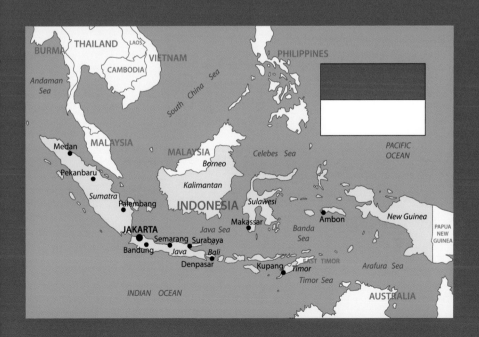

DAY 40: MISSIONARIES

AChristian missionary is someone who is sent by God to tell people about Jesus and show them his love through serving them in different ways. Often this involves moving to another country where the language and culture is different. Missionaries do different things such as starting a church, evangelism, teaching, medical work and building.

"'How beautiful is the person who comes to bring Good News.'" Romans 10:15

Missionaries and the people they are sharing their faith with need our prayers. In the Bible, Paul, the Apostle, was a missionary and he repeatedly asked believers to pray for him.

MEET CATHERINE

Catherine went to work as a missionary in Japan in 2011 shortly after the tragic tsunami happened there. She has been using a gift that God has given her by playing the harp to bring comfort to those who were affected by the tsunami. She is sharing about Jesus and seeing Japanese people respond to him. Catherine has had to face hard times and the difficult job of learning Japanese which is one of the hardest languages to learn. She has felt strengthened by God and encouraged by people in her church in the U.K. who have been praying for her and the people of Japan. She has seen many answers to their prayers.

DID YOU KNOW?

The Thai language has five tones so the same word can have different meanings when used with different tones! This can cause missionaries to make mistakes such as calling a mechanic an elephant!

PRAY

• For a missionary you know. For their children, health, safety in travel and help in language study. For the people they are reaching or helping to become Christians.

GET INTO IT!

* Choose a missionary to pray for. Get a photo of them and then make a regular time to pray for them. You can learn more about them and the work they are doing by reading their newsletters and finding out about the country where they live. You could also write a letter or email to them or their children so that you can get to know them better.

* Read about a famous missionary such as Helen Roseveare or Hudson Taylor.

INDEX:

The bold page numbers are the main sections for that country/topic, those numbers not in bold are the other places where that country/topic is referred to in the book.

Addictions	14, **60-61**
Afghanistan	**62-63**
Aviation Ministry	**26-27**
Bhutan	**58-59**
Brazil	**40-41**
Child Trafficking	**30-31**
Cities	**38-39**
Colombia	**36-37**
Creation Care	**34-35**
Diaspora	**84-85**
Egypt	**20-21**, 76
Europe	12, 44, **72-73**, 76
Floods	**22-23**, 34, 52
France	**44-45**
Greece	**12-13**
Greenland	**16-17**
Hinduism	58, **68-69**, 70, 80, 82
HIV/AIDS	**42-43**, 50
Homeless People	**14-15**, 38

Hui in China	**64-65**
Hunger	14, **46-47**, 14
Indonesia	80, **86-87**
Judaism	**56-57**
Madagascar	**8-9**
Maldives	**24-25**
Missionaries	8, 26, 27, 28, 40, 54, 72, 81, **88-89**
Nepal	68, **70-71**, 85
New Zealand	**66-67**
Orphans	**52-53**
Persecution	**18-19**, 82
Roma People	**76-77**
Saudi Arabia	**32-33**
Somalia	46, **78-79**
South Africa	26, **50-51**, 80
South Korea	**28-29**
Sri Lanka	24, **82-83**
The Gambia	**54-55**
Toilets	**10-11**
Unreached People Groups	62, 63, **80-81**, 87
Vietnam	**74-75**

THANKS

I would like to thank the following organisations for giving me permission to use their material:
Mission Aviation Fellowship [maf-uk.org] for kind permission to use their material for Mission Aviation
[Day 10]. If you want to know more about MAF, you could read 'Hope Has Wings' by Stuart King.
Open Doors for kind permission to use their material for Persecution [Day 6] and Somalia [Day 35].
Tearfund for kind permission to use their material sourced from www.tearfund.org for Child Trafficking
[Day 12] and Orphans [Day 22].
Toilet Twinning for kind permission to use their material for Toilets [Day 2].
Thank you also to Catherine Porter [Missionaries], Joseph Parkes [Diaspora], Mi Ran Tanner [The
Gambia], Shely Ganguly [Hinduism] and Steve King [Addictions] for permission to use their stories.

IMAGE CREDITS

Toilets (p.11) :	Used by permission of Toilet Twinning
Homeless People (p.15):	CarGe/Shutterstock.com
Persecution (p.19):	Zoltan Zempleni/Shutterstock.com
Open Doors logo (p.19):	Used by permission of Open Doors
Floods (p.23):	Laboo Studio/Shutterstock.com
Aviation Ministry (p.27):	Used by permission of MAF
Child Trafficking (p.31):	Eakachai Leesin/Shutterstock.com
'No Child Taken' logo (p.31):	Used by permission of Tearfund
Creation Care (p.35):	Evan Lorne/Shutterstock.com
Cities (p. 39):	aon168/Shutterstock.com
HIV/AIDS (p.43):	Sur/Shutterstock.com
Hunger (p.47):	africa924/Shutterstock.com
Orphans (p.53):	Danilo Mongiello/Dreamstime.com
Judaism (p.57):	Maksim Dubinsky/Shutterstock.com
Addictions (p. 61):	Used by permission of Steve King
Hui in China (p. 65):	TonyV3112/Shutterstock.com
Hinduism (p.69):	szefei/Shutterstock.com
Europe (p.73):	Lisa Kolbasa/Shutterstock.com
Europe map (p. 73)	Pasha_Barabonov/Shutterstock.com
Roma People (p.77):	dinosmichail/Shutterstock.com
Unreached People Groups (p.81):	COMIBAM/Sepal [via Joshua Project]
Diaspora (p.85):	Used by permission of Christine Cross
Missionaries (p.89):	Used by permission of Catherine Porter
Flags [on all country pages]:	Christophe Testi/Shutterstock.com
Maps [on all country pages except Greenland]:	pavalena/Shutterstock.com
Greenland map (p.17):	Peter Hermes Furian/Shutterstock.com
Front cover image (p.1, 2 & 3)	Lucie Drobna/Shutterstock.com
Centre maps (p. 48 & 49)	Pasha_Barabonov/Shutterstock.com

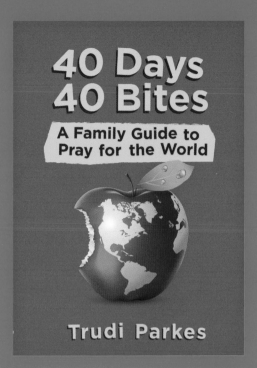

ISBN: 978-1-78191-401-4

40 Days 40 Bites:
A Family Guide to Pray for the World

This is a book that demands to be read and used in our
ministry of prayer for the nations... I will be making use of
this prayer guide in my own prayer ministry. Let's work hard
together to get this guide out and to get people to really
make use of it.

George Verwer, Founder and Former International Director,
Operation Mobilisation, Kent, England

In 40 tasty, easily digestible bites you can travel round God's
amazing world and pray! This book covers over twenty
different countries including Algeria, China, and North Korea.
It covers a variety of issues such as poverty, clean water and
translation. This family guide to praying for the world will
open your eyes to the need and challenge you to come before
God and pray

COUNTRY PRAYER REMINDERS

Tick each day once you've prayed for that country.

Madagascar

Greece

Greenland

Egypt

Maldives

South Korea

Saudi Arabia

Colombia

Brazil

France

South Africa

The Gambia

Bhutan

Afghanistan

New Zealand

Nepal

Vietnam

Somalia

Sri Lanka

Indonesia

TOPIC PRAYER REMINDERS

Tick each day once you've prayed for that topic/issue.

Toilets ⬭

Homeless People ⬭

Persecution ⬭

Floods ⬭

Aviation Ministry ⬭

Child Trafficking ⬭

Creation Care ⬭

Cities ⬭

HIV/AIDS ⬭

Hunger ⬭

Orphans ⬭

Judaism ⬭

Addictions ⬭

Hui in China ⬭

Hinduism ⬭

Europe ⬭

Roma People ⬭

Unreached People Groups ⬭

Diaspora ⬭

Missionaries ⬭

Christian Focus Publications publishes books for adults and children under its four main imprints: Christian Focus, CF4K, Mentor and Christian Heritage. Our books reflect our conviction that God's Word is reliable and Jesus is the way to know him, and live for ever with him.

Our children's publication list includes a Sunday School curriculum that covers pre-school to early teens, and puzzle and activity books. We also publish personal and family devotional titles, biographies and inspirational stories that children will love.

If you are looking for quality Bible teaching for children then we have an excellent range of Bible stories and age-specific theological books. From pre-school board books to teenage apologetics, we have it covered!

Find us at our web page: www.christianfocus.com

WORLD CHANGERS

World Changers is a network of Christian mission organisations including WEC, OMF and OM. They work together in London and South East England organising events to encourage people to get involved in world mission.

Follow them	Online	worldchangers.me.uk
	Twitter	WorldChangersEvents@worldchgevts
	Facebook	facebook.com/worldchangers.me.uk